What Every Pastor Should Know

What Every Pastor Should Know

7 Steps to a Spiritual Makeover

by

GARY HAWKINS, SR.

Published for

GARY HAWKINS MINISTRIES

NILES, ILLINOIS

Gary Hawkins Ministries
P.O. Box 870989
Stone Mountain, Georgia 30087
770.498.5850
Email: vof@voicesfaith.org

DEDICATION

This book is dedicated to the Holy Trinity for giving me the anointing, wisdom and boldness to write a book that will help pastors grow in the kingdom for God.

This book is also dedicated to pastors and leaders who are struggling in their faith to grow a great church for God. In order for these principles to become effective, they must be implemented.

I am also dedicating this book to my wife, and partner in ministry, Debbie E. Hawkins. Through her love and commitment she has joined me in kingdom work for God. This book is also dedicated to my four children, Elaina, Ashley, Gary Jr., and Kalen. Thank you for never giving up on me! I love you VERY MUCH!!!

This book is dedicated to my staff for making me look good! Your tenacity and commitment has pushed me to go to a new level with God.

Finally, this book is dedicated to my mother, Mary Louise Robertson. Thank you for raising me up to fear God and to never look down on people unless I am picking them up.

Gary Hawkins, Sr.

TABLE OF CONTENTS

ACKNOWLEDGMENTS

To my God, for doing what You do best, I love you with all my heart, soul, and mind! For allowing me to wake up each morning in my right mind; for imparting wisdom and direction through the Holy Spirit, I exhort Your name! And for loving me in spite of my handicaps, I praise You continually! I am sold out for You!

To the love of my life, Debbie Elaine Hawkins, you are the air I breathe! Because of you, I have become a better husband, a better father, a better pastor, most of all, a better person. Thank you for being my best friend!

To my wonderful four children, Elaina, Ashley, Gary Jr., and Kalen, where would I be without your love in my life? Again, I know it sounds like a broken record, but thank you for unselfishly sharing me with others.

To my mother, Mary L. Robertson, my love for you is unconditional. I don't have enough room in this book to describe how much you mean to me. Your prayers are working. I am on course to my destiny!

To my mother-n-love, Elzina Owens, favor reigns over your entire life! Because of you, God has allowed me to tap into the favor on your life. I love you tremendously!

I wish to express special acknowledgement and gratitude to Angia Levels. I am a better pastor because of you. I am a better author because of you. Your faithfulness has not gone unnoticed.

Thank you for all the things I don't often mention to you. I love you for your unwavering commitment to excellence!

Valerie Murkison, you are absolutely awesome! You have exhausted yourself, family, and time to assist me to build the kingdom. I love you very very much! Thank you for your countless hours in assisting me to write this book.

To my brother and sister-n-love, Aaron and Mia Hawkins, no one does it better than the two of you. Your unwavering love and commitment has been unsurpassed. To the rest of my family, Walter, John, Reginald, Denita, Wayne, Aldreamer, Mary, Warren, Victorina, Chris, Theresa, Gladys, Ann, Gail, Shelia, Dwight, Andrea, Michael, Roy, and Judy, God could not have sent a more loving family.

To Earl, Jasper, Paula, and Theresa thank you for believing in Debbie and I. We are always praying for your success.

To my nieces, nephews, cousins, and friends, too many to name, you know I love you and appreciate your love and prayers!

To my pastoral staff, Lorraine Dykes, whose work efforts are unmatched, my nephew, Tyrone Lane, Barbara Jones, James Murkison, Althea Brooks, Lakisha Chatman, Quiana Rosemond, Kathleen Dunning, Neva Romaine, Cynthia Ward, David Ferebee, Dewaine Johnson, Zenda Duren, Laura Walker, Shawnea Barry, Taronda Crouth-Durant, Debran Adams, Yvette Green, Bernadette Stockard and Collard Alexander. I would not trade you for all the tea in China. Thank you for bringing your "A" game every single day. You are the reason our ministry walks in a spirit of excellence.

Finally, I would like to thank each pastor and leader for taking the time to read this book. You have been called by God to grow a great church for the kingdom and this book was written with you in mind. My desire is that the material contained on every page be a blessing to those who implement it.

FOREWORD

This book, "What Every Pastor Should Know!" is a must read! This book is destined to take your ministry to the next dimension. Bishop Gary Hawkins, Sr. creates a spiritual atmosphere designed to destroy old traditions hindering the church from moving into kingdom principles. The body of Christ has longed awaited a book of this magnitude that would give Godly principles and simplistic tools to assist pastors and lay leaders alike to grow a great church for the kingdom. This book has the right ingredients that pastors need to grow a healthy church. The seven principles found in chapter one alone will help give your church the "Spiritual Makeover" it desperately needs to go to the next level.

Fasten your seat belts! Your flight is now on the runway and you have been cleared for takeoff. This flight will change your ministry forever! Turbulence and delays have slowed your ministry down in the past, but after reading this book, your ministry will soar over rough air and traffic jams found at the lower levels of ministry. Bishop Hawkins mesmerizes you with thought-provoking truths that will push you into your destiny.

Pay close attention to chapter five, "Me Time." This chapter is designed to bless the busy pastor who has forgotten to take care of his/her needs. I believe stress has not only weakened the pastor, but the church as well. Our environment would be less stressful if more pastors took time to pamper themselves with massages and other relaxing things. The result, more souls would be reached for the kingdom of heaven.

I am often in awe of God! When I look at Bishop Hawkins and Voices of Faith Ministries, it reminds me of New Birth several years ago. A church very few in the city knew about, but now the world is discovering the hand of God on their ministry. God is no respecter of a person. Applying these Godly principles found in this book to your ministry will push your church closer to its destiny.

If you desire to grow a great church in the kingdom, "What Every Pastor Should Know" is the book I highly recommend! This book has all the necessary tools to equip your ministry. In the words of my favorite expression, "Watch This!" Your life is about to be radically changed for the kingdom.

Eddie L. Long,
Bishop, New Birth Missionary Baptist Church,
Lithonia, Georgia

INTRODUCTION

During my teenage years, growing up in Baton Rouge, Louisiana my friends and I would go swimming in lakes and ponds around the city. At the time, there were very few opportunities to swim at the YMCA and other recreational parks. I could not swim, but I would go along for the fun. I often would find shallow water in which to play. One particular hot summer day, my friends and I decided to go to a new pond to swim. All of my friends was jumping off the edge into the water and climbing back upon the bank to do it again. I remember playing with them as if I was going to jump, but I never had any intentions of really jumping. As I got closer to the edge, the slippery embankment gave way under my feet as I slid into the pond. I was screaming for help, but to no avail. Every one in the pond watched with excitement and laughter. Finally, someone yelled, "Gary, just stand up!" To my amazement, the water was only to my knees. From the top of the embankment, it appeared as if the water was ten feet deep, but in actuality, we were swimming in shallow water.

Many pastors have suffered from growing a great church because they have refused to jump head first into the water. From your vantage point, the water is too deep and over your head. Like me, as a teenager, your desire is only to play on the embankment. God's desire is for you to jump into the deepest part of the pond knowing you will have to depend on Him to survive.

My reason for writing this book is to yell, "Just stand up!" Take your rightful place in the kingdom and be accounted for. The water is not as deep as it seems from the surface. God is testing your faith. He wants to know whether or not you will remain on the embankment or get in the water and get your feet wet.

I pray that through the reading of this book, you gain the courage to jump into the deepest part of the pond. God has a desire to see your ministry grow. Trust God as your life jacket and watch Him sail you to shore safely.

CHAPTER 1

SEVEN PRINCIPLES
FOR A SPIRITUAL MAKEOVER

A spiritual makeover is a set of God given principles designed to overhaul your ministry and push it toward the destiny that God desires for your life. Godly principles will work in any environment and in any situation. These principles will work for the saved and unsaved. They are no respecter of a person. **Matthew 5:45** says, *"That ye may be the children of your Father which is in heaven: for he maketh his sun to rise on the evil and on the good, and sendeth rain on the just and on the unjust."* We are often in search of answers from God to help jumpstart our ministries. God desires to bless your ministry, but you oftentimes refuse to let go of yesterday. You are still holding on to things that have been

Your church is in need of a spiritual makeover!

1

dead in your life for years. Every time God moves you forward three steps, you turn and look back on the way your ministry operated in your father's day and walk backwards five steps. God is trying to take you where you have never gone before, but your faith has to trust Him so that He may get the glory. Your church is in need of a spiritual makeover! Therefore, I am about to share with you seven principles for a spiritual makeover that will transform your ministry and bring it to the forefront, so that you may take over your city for the kingdom of God.

PRINCIPLE ONE: DEVELOP A GIVING SPIRIT

Giving is contagious! It is one of the prime reasons our ministry has exploded with church growth. We have developed a giving spirit. We developed this principle from watching God. God is the Master Giver. **John 3:16-17** says, *"(16) For God so loved the world, that he gave his only begotten Son, that whosoever believeth in him should not perish, but have everlasting life. (17) For God sent not his Son into the world to condemn the world; but that the world through him might be saved."* I am forever grateful to God for sending His Son, Jesus Christ into the world to save a sinner like me. I believe if I was the only sinner on the face of the earth, God would have still sent Jesus to die for me. God is the Master Giver.

Learn how to give openly before your congregation so they

can see your heart and love for their families. Too many churches are constantly begging their members to give for one reason after another, but the members never see the church blessing others in need. I am not saying we should not teach and encourage our members to tithe and serve the Lord faithfully. I am only saying we should not always have our hands out waiting for them to bless the church. It is time for the church to be a blessing to the people as well. It is time for the church to show some generosity.

In August 2005, New Orleans, Louisiana and the coastal cities of Mississippi were devastated from the disaster of Hurricane Katrina. Thousands of people lost their lives, homes, and all of their possessions. In a span of 24 hours, Hurricane Katrina changed the future of millions of people. Many are scattered from their families and homeland. Churches and businesses alike were under water. Dead bodies were floating in the water. The homes of the people of New Orleans and the coastal cities of Mississippi were demolished from Hurricane Katrina. New Orleans looked like a war zone. Families were rooted up from their birth place only to be forced to live in strange cities and in shelters not knowing how they would ever recover. Over 200,000 evacuees from New Orleans, the surrounding Louisiana cities, and the Gulf Coast of Mississippi fled to Atlanta, Georgia. Their livelihood as they knew it, no longer existed. Many shelters have worked overtime to assist them with food and personal hygiene items. Churches, businesses, and other nonprofit organizations alike have done an excellent job of providing food and clothing.

Immediately after Hurricane Katrina ripped through New Orleans and the coastal cities of Mississippi, I began to pray and ask God to show me what we could do to make a difference in a few families' lives. My prayer was answered immediately. Deacon Gregory B. Levett, one of my best friends and mentors in the body of Christ called and said, "Pastor, God told me to tell you that Voices of Faith Ministries need to place families in an apartment and pay their rent for a few months." I immediately received the Word from the Lord and responded. We placed three families in an apartment complex for six months free of charge. We paid all of their utilities; electricity, gas, and water. We even paid for their local telephone service. We only wanted the families to focus on rebuilding their lives and looking for a job without any added stress. When I announced to our congregation what God laid on my heart to do for three families, they erupted with joy, praise, and excitement! It had a ricochet affect. Everyone joined in and assisted in this vision. We were not holding our hands out looking for a blessing, but we stepped up and publicly announced to our congregation that for six months we will be a blessing to others in their time of need. We must learn how to openly give before our congregations so they can see our heart.

Every year we have given scholarships to high school seniors assisting them with their books and tuition. We have assisted members with their mortgages and rents. We have created businesses within our church and empowered our members with jobs.

Believe it or not, we have even paid off debt for some of our members. **Luke 6:38** says, *"Give, and it shall be given unto you; good measure, pressed down, and shaken together, and running over, shall men give into your bosom..."* The moment you develop a giving spirit, is the moment God overtakes you with blessings.

In my own personal life, I have developed this principle. I have seen God do tremendous things for my family because of this principle. Every month, my wife, Debbie and I send our parents, Mary Louise Robertson and Elzina Owens a generous gift of love. I continually bless staff members with love offerings just to say thank you for being a great blessing to me and my family. Oftentimes at the dinner table with friends and other pastors, I insist on paying for the meal because I know God will give me in return much more than a meal, but favor beyond my wildest dreams. Oh Yes! I have a giving spirit. My mother said, "Gary, because of your generosity towards me, you have stretched me to give even more to others." My mother often takes the love offerings that I give her and sow it into other places. She told me that she was using a portion of the blessing for the month of September 2005 to sow into a shelter that will assist Hurricane Katrina victims. If you want to take your ministry to the next level, then you must develop a giving spirit and master this principle.

PRINCIPLE TWO:
DEVELOP A TRANSPARENT SPIRIT

I believe this principle to be the most critical of them all. Principle two reveals your character. It even exposes your motives. Too many pastors are constantly hiding information from their congregation. They have been taught to be secretive. I believe many people in the congregation refuse to give God their best because they believe their pastors are also cheating God.

In January 2005, I taught a four week financial series at my church. This was the very first time I had ever taught a series on finances in my eleven years of pastorate. I told my congregation that after the teaching on finances was finished to bring their best seed offering to the Lord on the first Sunday of February 2005. Sow where you want God to take you! I told them that the money would be used to pay off all of the bills at our church. I showed them a view of our debt on a power point spreadsheet. They were able to see the breakdown of our finances. I did not hide anything from them. I told them that when we take care of God's house, God is obligated to take care of our houses. I became very transparent with them. I shared how much tithe and offering my wife and I gave to the church last year and that we believed God would double it the next year. I shared my heart. Our desire is that God allows our offering to supersede our

> ## Sow where you want God to take you!

tithe. We truly want to bless the Lord with our whole heart. Debbie and I also shared the amount of our seed offering with our congregation. We said, "God spoke to us to sow $15,000 and we were going to be obedient." The moment my wife and I became transparent with them, it seems as if heaven broke over our ministry. Countless numbers of people began to stand in the congregation to tell what they were sowing to the Lord. One couple said, "Pastor we are going to match your $15,000." Another said, "God is speaking to us to give $5,000." The entire church became contagious about giving. Why? Because we were willing to be open and transparent about our seed, our congregation felt a need to share their seed offering to the Lord. On the first Sunday in February 2005, we raised approximately $600,000. Praise The Lord!

Recently, I received a check of $15,000 from a business deal. I shared it with my congregation. I told them that I will not deposit the check into my savings account, but will turn it over to the church so they can use the money to buy a third camera for the ministry. I even shared with them that Debbie and I would purchase a boom camera for the church. The cost of the boom camera was $10,000. I truly believe out of my willingness to be transparent, God continues to provide every step of the way.

A faithful member served our ministry tirelessly. Recently, she announced she was moving to Richmond, Virginia to be close to her family. It broke my heart to see her leave our ministry. She understood how to serve in the kingdom. I announced it to the church that she was leaving and that we would bless her with a check of $1,000 for being so faithful. After receiving the offering, she pays her tithe and then gives Debbie and I a check for $100 a piece. She said, "Pastor, I need to sow into you and Elder Debbie." She has been the blessing to me and yet she wanted to sow into us. God is an awesome God! The moment you develop a transparent spirit, nothing will stop you from receiving God's best. Your members have to see you being the example. When they see your heart and giving spirit, it causes them to sow as well.

PRINCIPLE THREE:
DEVELOP A CONFRONTATIONAL SPIRIT

Most pastors and leaders need an emergency course in this principle. We oftentimes feel if we don't address issues in our church, the problems will solve itself over a period of time. When we allow problems to fester over a period of time, the situation escalates like a wild fire in a hot desert. When we refuse to address issues and people causing the problems in our church, cancer spreads rapidly throughout the congregation mostly affecting innocent people.

> **Our job is to confront those that could destroy our ministry.**

My philosophy, "I would rather lose one person or a small group of people in my church, rather than the entire church." If we are to grow a healthy church, we must develop a confrontational spirit. A confrontational spirit does not mean that we are to confront every issue in the church. Some issues are brush fires and do not need immediate attention.

A couple of years ago, a popular minister in my church, who was also one of my Sunday School teachers, was having weekly bible study at his home with about fifteen other members: including ministers and deacons. This went on for months without my knowledge. Over a period of time, he sent me a letter expressing his unhappiness about the ministry. He shared that he did not enjoy my teaching, leadership style, and philosophy about the Word of God. He also mentioned, that he was stepping down as minister and was going to find a church that ministered to his needs and fit his philosophy. I respect a man who voices his opinion. I had no grudges. I wished him and his family great success in the future. I was not angry because I understood I will not please everyone in ministry. A week later, he showed up at the church to teach Sunday School. One of my members came and told me that he was currently teaching in the Sunday School class. I told my security team to immediately stop him from teaching. I told them that he was no longer allowed to teach another word at this church. I respected his opinion, but he could not teach at this church with a different philosophy than mine. I refused to wait until he finished teaching the class. I knew I had to make a statement to him and any others who would test my leadership for the kingdom. I knew that I was going to lose a few people. I knew a small group of leaders would also leave with him. Moments after I stopped him from teaching and announced to the Sunday school class that he was no longer allowed to teach, at our church, a few members who were followers of his teaching immediately left to never return. Every single member of his weekly Bible Study eventually left our ministry over a period time. Some left our church sooner than others. Our job is to confront those that could destroy our ministry. God is amazing! When they left our church, God raised the ministry to another level and He raised me to another dimension in leadership. God was waiting on me to confront people that did not have my heart and His vision.

PRINCIPLE FOUR: DON'T EMPOWER THOSE WHO DON'T HAVE YOUR HEART

Why do we place the wrong people in charge? We often place people in charge of important ministries in our church for the wrong reasons. We place people in charge who often have bad attitudes. Do not empower those who will be jealous of your every move. Place people in charge of key roles in your ministry that will celebrate your success. When you buy a new house, they should rejoice

Place people in charge of key roles in your ministry that will celebrate your success.

10

that God is blessing you. Your blessing is an indication that the line is moving. Their mindset should be, if God is blessing the pastor then I can expect for my blessing to come shortly. Most people don't leave the church because of you; most people leave the church because who you have empowered. I cannot tell you over the course of pastorship these eleven years how many people have left our church because of a leader I had in charge over a key ministry who really did not have my heart.

A year ago, a key ministry in our church was losing members and losing them fast. Over a period of time I noticed that this ministry was dying and it seemed as if life had been sucked out of the ministry. Some who served in this ministry were even leaving our church. I began to ask each and every one of them why were they not serving in this ministry? I shared with them that God's desire for them was to utilize their gifts and talents for the Lord. They began to share that the ministry was no longer fun. Some even said, "Coming to church feels like a chore and not something I am excited about." After further investigating the ministry, I found out that the leaders did not have my heart and vision. I confronted them to strive for excellence for the Lord, but my words fell on deaf ear. Shortly thereafter, the ministry furthered deteriorated. A few weeks later, they resigned from the church. The very next week, after announcing their resignation to the congregation, that ministry doubled in attendance. That ministry is now thriving for the Lord! What was the difference? We replaced our old leaders who did not have my heart with new leaders who have my heart and vision. The results were remarkable! A change of leadership created instant success.

PRINCIPLE FIVE:
DEVELOP A PROGRESSIVE SPIRIT

Many pastors lack this principle. Too many pastors are laid back in ministry. All they want to do is preach the Word of God. We spend countless number of hours in the mirror working on our sermon, but very little attention and time is focused on reaching the people's need through the week. Great preaching doesn't grow great churches. You must develop leaders around you to help grow your church. Great ideas come from leaders around you who have your heart and vision. These are leaders you have given the authority to dream and strategize ways to take your ministry to the next level.

> God has given you everything you need to be successful in the body of Christ.

You must develop a progressive spirit! I need to repeat this sentence again. You must develop a progressive spirit! You can not allow life to hit you and knock you down. You must get up off the first punch. Quit waiting on things to happen. You must make them happen! Quit using excuses in the pulpit! Quit telling your congregation that you are not going to move ahead until you hear from God. You will not hear from God until you move ahead. Quit letting the pulpit handicap you. God has given you everything you need to be successful in the body of Christ. You must utilize the tools and gifts around you.

Recently, we broke ground to build a new church in our second location of Rockdale County, Georgia. The building project is scheduled for completion Spring of 2006. We are currently holding our Sunday morning worship service at a local middle school in Rockdale County until our church edifice is complete. Our goal is to fill up the auditorium NOW! We do not want to wait until we move in our new church edifice before we start attracting the unchurched. I knew I needed drastic measures to make an impact in Rockdale County. Our church was new in the county and no one knew who we were. I knew Voices of Faith Ministries had to make a bold statement. We had to be extremely progressive! We placed five billboards in Rockdale County and we placed one billboard ad in their movie theater. Why, because I am going to take the city for the kingdom of God. I cannot be passive. I must be extremely progressive. Every major street you drive on in Rockdale County, there is a picture of one of our billboards. I don't want the people to think of anything else but Voices of Faith Ministries. Our goal is to saturate the market to bring exposure to our ministry. We want our church to stay on the mind of the people in Rockdale County.

We have over twelve billboards all over metropolitan Atlanta. Our television broadcast is aired locally three times a week. Our broadcast is also shown in over 35 million homes in the United

States and in over 100 million homes in over 50 countries. We also air our television broadcast in Baton Rouge and Lake Charles, Louisiana and in Beaumont, Texas twice a week. We send out over 4,000 postcards a month to new homeowners. We are extremely progressive and yet I am still not satisfied.

My friend, Dr. Zachery Tims who pastors New Destiny Christian Center in Orlando, Florida also knows a thing or two about progressiveness. He has over 25 billboards in the city of Orlando. He comes on local television everyday of the week. His radio program in Orlando also comes on daily. His television broadcast is shown on The Word Network everyday in over 35 million homes in the United States and over 100 million homes worldwide. I am not surprised that he is taking his city.

It is not enough to perfect your sermons for Sunday mornings. We must find creative ways to reach the masses. The moment you develop a progressive spirit, is the moment your ministry will change.

PRINCIPLE SIX:
DEVELOP A SPIRIT OF EXCELLENCE

I believe if we are to see a move of God take place in our ministries, we must first develop a spirit of excellence in our churches. The size of your ministry does not matter; give God your very best at that level. It does not matter whether or not you are worshipping in a store front, a movie theater, or a school auditorium, show God excellence!

In August 1994 when we first started in ministry, we had very little money, but a great vision to serve the people and do the will of God. I had one criteria and that was to serve God with excellence at the level we were. I remember producing fliers to pass out in the community introducing our ministry and promoting our Sunday morning worship service. We produced the best flier we could afford at that time. We could not afford colored fliers, but no one could have done a better job pro-

> **The worst thing is to do a half-hearted job for the kingdom.**

ducing black and white. We were a small church, but we served a big God. We may have been small, but we never thought small. I believe God has honored us by allowing us to grow a great church because we always gave Him our best.

The worst thing is to do a half-hearted job for the kingdom. My slogan is: "If you cannot do it right, leave it alone." Too many churches are producing church programs and bulletins that are embarrassing. Remember, your name is on your work. John Maxwell once said, "You will never attract who you want, but you will attract who you are." If you want to attract excellence in your church, start operating in excellence. Everybody wants to be associated with a winner. Start being that winner NOW!

God wants excellence! Cain and Abel faced this same dilemma. **Genesis 4:3-5** says, *"(3) And in process of time it came to pass, that Cain brought of the fruit of the ground an offering unto the LORD. (4) And Abel, he also brought of the firstlings of his* *flock and of the fat thereof. And the LORD had respect unto Abel and to his offering. (5) But unto Cain and to his offering he had not respect. And Cain was very wroth, and his countenance fell.* "

God was pleased with Abel's offering because he gave God his very best. Abel gave God a spirit of excellence! On the other hand, God was disappointed with Cain's offering because he gave God leftovers. The results were simple, Abel prospered beyond measures and Cain suffered. Cain became jealous of Abel's success and murdered his brother. Just walk in excellence and watch God bless your ministry.

PRINCIPLE SEVEN: PULL OUT YOUR SECRET WEAPON

This seventh principle may be the most powerful of them all. Using your secret weapon will take your church to another dimension. Pastors, your secret

It is time to reveal your secret weapon to the world.

weapon has been hidden too long in your churches. It is time to reveal your secret weapon to the world. This secret weapon can also be utilized to help fight our enemies. Our secret weapon is our wives. That's right! Our wives have so much influence and power in the church, but pastors have tried to keep them hidden from the public's view. Many women admire the first lady to the point where they start to dress like her and take on her attributes. First

16

Lady Debbie has experienced many women in our church approaching her to say how much they admire her. Many have said, "They want to be like her some day." First Ladies have so much influence in the church. They just need a platform to be heard. God designed them to walk with us, yet many pastors keep their precious wives hidden to shield them from trouble. **Genesis 2:18** – *"And the LORD God said, It is not good that the man should be alone; I will make him an help meet for him."* Our wives were designed to walk with us to grow a great church for the Lord.

Debbie and I do everything together in ministry. We are pictured together on billboards across the metropolitan city of Atlanta. Even though I have written several books, Debbie's picture is included on the back of each book. On our weekly television broadcast, Debbie and I record the opening and closing remarks for each broadcast. I am no fool, my wife is beautiful. She makes me look good on television. I am often amazed that when we are out in public together, many people will not recognize me even though I am on television doing 99% of the preaching. As soon as they see Debbie's face, they look back at me and say, "Now, I have seen you on television. I recognize you by your wife." Praise the Lord! I tell Debbie all the time, I am just glad to be in her company.

Some of the largest churches in our country are ministries who give the first lady an opportunity to be seen and heard. Pastor Joel Osteen and his wife, Victoria from Houston, Texas can be seen all over the world together on his weekly television broadcast. Bishop T.D. Jakes and his wife, Serita from Dallas, Texas are often seen on television together. My mentor, Dr. I.V. Hilliard and his wife, Dr. Bridgett from Houston, Texas often rotate preaching assignments. My good friends Pastor Dwayne Pickett and his wife, Traci from Jackson, Mississippi minister together. Another great friend of mine Pastor Getties Jackson and his wife, Anita from Greer, South Carolina work hand in hand together in ministry. Pastor Zachery Tims and his wife, Riva from Orlando, Florida often tag team together. Dr. Michael Freeman and his wife, Dr. Dee Dee from Temple Hills, Maryland often share the same pulpit on Sundays. My big brother in ministry, Pastor Raymond W. Johnson and his wife, Mildred from Baton Rouge, Louisiana have excelled together in ministry. Dr. Creflo Dollar and his wife, Taffi from Atlanta, Georgia are teaching the Word of God on television everyday in almost every city in America. My good friends Drs. Ben and Jewel Tankard tag team on Sunday mornings and share a weekly broadcast in Nashville, Tennessee. My good friends Bishop Larry Manning and his wife, Dr. Angela from Valdosta, Georgia rotate preaching assignments twice a month. Even my spiritual father, Bishop Eddie Long and his wife, Vanessa from Lithonia, Georgia are enjoying ministry together more than ever. Finally, Pastors Randy and Paula White from Tampa, Florida share the pulpit together at their church. These are just a few of the many successful pastors around the world that are doing great ministry at a whole new level. They all have excelled in ministry because they discovered the secret weapon was their wives. Pastors, I encourage you to give your wife a platform and a voice in the church and watch your ministry soar like eagles.

I admit some first ladies may not be ready for the public's eye. I do not recommend that you force her into the spot light without her consent. But I do encourage you to equip her and develop her speaking and communication skills to help assist you in ministry. Pastors, a first lady is able to reach a group of people in your church you will never be able to reach.

Many pastors have kept their wives hidden because we have been taught to keep her quiet and out of the way in the traditional church. Growing up in church, I never saw the first lady participate in any activities. She would show up on Sunday mornings and take her seat in a certain spot in the church and look good. The old school church forbids the first lady from participating in any functions. Oftentimes, she was miserable in the church because she felt left out of all important decision-making.

As you share your wife with the church, you will also discover that she can help ease your load. Sometimes when I have to leave and go minister at other churches, I feel good knowing Debbie is at our church to take up the slack from where I left off. Recently, I preached a sermon describing how tithes and offering work. Debbie assisted me with the entire sermon. We received so many calls from around the country and in our church expressing their joy and love of seeing Debbie and I minister together. The moment you unleash your secret weapon, your current seating capacity in your church may be too small to hold the people that God will send.

Finally, encourage your first lady to fellowship with other first ladies that are co-laboring with their husbands in ministry. My wife has written a book entitled *What Every First Lady Should Know* and this book is a must read for your wife. God has also anointed her to reach the hearts of first ladies and equip them for their calling. By the way, she has written another book entitled *From the Hearts of First Ladies*, which will be a tremendous blessing to your wife. Once a year Debbie hosts a sleep over for select first ladies and they fellowship and spend a weekend being empowered, encouraged and getting refreshed. God has blessed me to become the spiritual father to over sixty pastors and growing rapidly. I encourage the pastors to include their spouses in everything we do. Twice a year Debbie and I host a summit for this ministry called the "Eagles Nest" and we fellowship with them together and we breakout into sessions and speak with them individually. I am starting to spiritually father more female pastors; therefore, we will have to be creative on speaking to the first men as well.

CHAPTER 1
FOR DISCUSSION

1. What are the seven principles for a spiritual makeover?
   1. _____
   2. _____
   3. _____
   4. _____
   5. _____
   6. _____
   7. _____

2. Why is it so important to overhaul a ministry stuck in neutral?

3. How can a giving spirit unlock lack in your life?

4. What effects will a transparent spirit have on a congregation? Explain.

5. When is the right time to be confrontational? Explain.

6. What would happen if you empowered someone who did not have your spirit? Explain.

7. List five things that you do in your church that is a spirit of excellence.
   1. _____
   2. _____
   3. _____
   4. _____
   5. _____

8. Why is it important to include your wife in ministry? Explain.

CHAPTER 2

THE PEP RALLY INVITATION

I am excited about a lot of material and pertinent information in this book that you will learn to help grow your ministry, but "The Pep Rally Invitation" may just top them all. I kind of stumbled upon this principle. Praise the Lord! "The Pep Rally Invitation" is the highlight of my Sunday morning worship service. Pastors, if you want immediate results, this principle will work in your church as soon as you apply

Your ministry is about to soar to new heights overnight.

it. There is a catch. You must have people visiting your church for this to be effective. It does not matter whether your church has twenty members or five thousand, this principle will work. It does not matter whether or not your church is on the east, south, north, or west coast, the principles will explode your church. It does not matter whether or not your church is in the inner city, suburbs, or the country, apply this principle and you will have to build a larger edifice. If you are ready to begin, I need your undivided attention. Your ministry is about to soar to new heights overnight.

I believe the reason our ministries suffer new growth each Sunday is because we spend all of our attention and energy on the sermon itself and not the "Call For Discipleship." The "Call For Discipleship" is an opportunity in the worship service for sinners and the unchurched to give their lives to Jesus Christ as Lord and Saviour. For the sake of this writing, I will rename "Call For Discipleship" to "The Pep Rally Invitation." I am not saying your preparation time for your sermon is not important, but I am saying we do not spend enough time on the "Pep Rally Invitation." It is like a fisherman who spends countless hours preparing the bait for the fish, but once the fish bites the bait on the hook he has no idea how to pull it in. His energy and preparation was only on the bait, not on how to pull in the fish. I believe few people are joining our churches today because all of our attention has only been on the preaching aspect of the worship service.

Another reason we suffer with new growth in our churches is the way we handle the call to discipleship. We often embarrass potential new members. We frighten them with our old school approach to ministry. There are many people that have a desire to come forward and join your church, but they are afraid that you would put them on the spot before the congregation. Please don't embarrass them before the congregation and ask their name. Every Sunday you are leaving a large group of unchurched people unsaved because of the way you have done your invitation.

The "Pep Rally Invitation" is the most important time of the worship service. How you handle the invitation can determine the success of your ministry. Many traditional churches extend the invitation by asking people who do not have a relationship with God to give their lives to Jesus Christ by coming to the altar and publicly confessing Christ as Saviour. In front of the congregation, the pastor would ask each new member a series of questions concerning their salvation. He would ask questions such as: Are you saved? Have you given your life to Jesus Christ? Have you ever been baptized? Do you know the Lord as your personal Saviour? What's your name? Where are you from? Here's the dilemma with that process. The number one fear in the world is public speaking. Many people are afraid to speak before large crowds; therefore it hinders the growth of your church when questions are asked in public before the congregation. We must remember that our goal is to reach the unchurched, not run them away. Rick Warren, author of *The Purpose-Driven Church* said, "Since the church is a living organism, it is natural for it to grow if it is healthy. The church is a body, not a business. It is an organism, not an organization. It is alive. If a church is not growing, it is dying."

I remember as a teenager being frightened to death when joining my church in Baton Rouge, Louisiana. After six months of procrastinating, I finally walked down the aisles with my knees shaking because I was afraid to speak before the church. I was terrified. I suggest you find a room in the church to minister to their needs.

At Voices of Faith, ministers, deacons and deaconess line up in the aisles and escort new members out of the sanctuary into a particular room in the church to minister to their needs without asking them embarrassing questions in public. There are trained ministers waiting in the rooms to determine their spiritual status with God. Now the new member can answer sensitive questions freely without the church listening to their every word, making it easier for new members to reach a decision.

Actually before they are escorted out of the sanctuary, each new member gets a hug. One of the most powerful weapons we possess is giving someone a hug. A hug breaks down stereotypes, barriers, and culture differences. When a new member decides Voices of Faith is where God has led them to join, elders, ministers, deacons, and deaconesses are waiting in the aisles to give each new member a hug. A hug is a powerful tool.

When you think of a pep rally, you think of high energy at a football or basketball game. A pep rally is designed to get people EXCITED about their favorite team. Cheerleaders and mascots are formed to get the players and fans alike excited about beating their opponents. The band also helps with the excitement by playing popular upbeat songs. The songs the band plays causes the players and fans energy level to soar to new heights.

Cheerleaders, mascots, and the band are your team leaders. They set the pace and excitement of the game. Cheerleaders and mascots help set the atmosphere for their teams to win. Fans in the stands wear war paint on their faces to show their support and intensity for their team. Many people lose their voices during the game because of the screaming and yelling for their favorite team. When our favorite team scores a touchdown or hit the winning basket, we erupt with joy and excitement. Sometimes the atmosphere is so loud you can barely hear yourself talk. We wear team colors to support our team. We place our favorite team flags on our cars to show support. We create an atmosphere conducive for winning.

What would happen if we set that kind of atmosphere in our churches? What would happen if we brought that kind of excitement to our personal invitations? What would happen if the congregation lost their minds with excitement when one soul got saved? What would happen if people shouted when drug dealers were delivered and prostitutes were cleansed by the Holy Spirit? A Revival would break out in our churches that would spill over into our cities. We would take our cities for the kingdom of God.

To effectively master the "Pep Rally Invitation" you must be energetic. Pastors, you are God's cheerleaders. Your job is to get the people fired up about saving souls. They must see your energy level. They must see your excitement. When you lead them in screaming and yelling they will follow suit. Many pastors lack enthusiasm in winning the lost to Christ. They don't expect anybody to join their churches. I expect at least thirty new members every Sunday. I expect God to move. He has ordained me to win souls for Jesus Christ. I expect nothing less than the best from God.

We must be animated about winning souls to Christ. Every time some one joins our church, I go wild. If I could turn cart-

wheels, I would. It is an exciting

We must be animated about winning souls to Christ.

time in the Lord. You get an opportunity to see people's lives change for the better. The church feeds off my energy and animation. When

they see me jumping and praising God, it gets them fired up to do the same.

We must be sincere. The worst thing to do when winning souls for Jesus Christ is to be phony. Phony people are spotted a mile a way. The congregation needs to see your heart. They need to know that you are sincere about seeing their lives change. I tell my congregation all the time that I love them and I am constantly praying for them. They feel the pulse from my heart and know that I am sincere and real with them.

You must get the congregation involved. Pastors, as a cheerleader in the church, your job is to find a creative way to get the congregation involved. I encourage the congregation to stand when the "Pep Rally Invitation" begins. Many churches sit during the call to discipleship. It causes the unchurched to hesitate about joining your church. Earlier I stated we place elders, ministers, deacons, and deaconess on each aisle and in the front of the pulpit with their arms extended waiting in great anticipation for new members. I stand in the pulpit encouraging the congregation to clap, shout, and run with excitement when a soul gets saved. We greet each new member with a hug. The crowd is going crazy and the atmosphere is contagious. When one person joins our church and the crowd is clapping and yelling from the top of their voices, it causes another individual to do the same. It is like a domino affect.

There must be a pep rally experience. I have had members in my church to tell me that the "Pep Rally Invitation" was so powerful that they almost joined church again. It is a wild time in the Lord! You must make it a memorable experience, one that the people would never forget. You must believe God's desire is to get folks saved. Giving your life to Jesus Christ is one of the most important things you will ever do in a lifetime.

You must have a room set up in the church to meet their needs. Once your potential members come down the aisle to join your church, they need to be escorted out of the sanctuary and into a private room to be led to Christ Jesus. This is very important. When other potential members see that you are not questioning them in front of the congregation, they will feel compelled to join your church as well. Many pastors place chairs in front of the church. This is a taboo. The chairs are placed in the front of the church so that the people in the congregation can see who have joined church. These chairs place God in a box. Your deacons put out one or two chairs and God wants to bring many down for salvation. It has become routine. The chairs will not work with the pep rally invitation. Remove the chairs at once! They also use that time to take their personal information. They find out who came down for salvation or who joined under Christian experience. All of this can be done in a room in the back of your church.

Pastors, read very carefully. This "Pep Rally Invitation" really works. All you have to do is try it. You have nothing to lose. Many of you have not seen a great harvest in your life. If this "Pep Rally Invitation" is done correctly, your results will be unbelievable! Many pastors all over the country, who have tried the "Pep Rally Invitation", have told me that their churches are exploding with growth. They were amazed that they did not have to change their preaching styles. They only had to change the way they extended their personal invitation for discipleship. I have used this approach for six years. Because of this principle, Voices of Faith has grown from 75 members six years ago to now over 7,000. Remember, God is no respecter of a person. What He does for one in principle, He will do the same for others. I can not wait to hear your results. It is time for you to take your city!

CHAPTER 2

FOR DISCUSSION

1. Do you feel the Pep Rally Invitation could work in your ministry? Explain.

2. How different is the Pep Rally Invitation from your current Call to Discipleship? Explain.

3. Why do so many people procrastinate when committing themselves to the Lord?

4. What is the number one fear in America?

5. How much energy and preparation should go into the Pep Rally Invitation? What would you do?

6. What is the purpose of the Pep Rally Invitation? What kind of atmosphere it creates? Explain.

7. Why should the pastor be energetic during the Pep Rally Invitation? Explain.

8. Why is it important to escort the new members out of the sanctuary during the Pep Rally Invitation?

CHAPTER 3

WHAT EVERY PASTOR
SHOULD KNOW

PLACE VISION STATEMENT ON EVERYTHING

lace your vision statement on everything. Everything!
Place your vision statement on all the doors of the sanctuary, all the doors in the office, the church's letterhead, website, T-shirts, bulletins, banners, marquee, etc…. It is crucial for your people to know the vision. **Habakkuk 2:2-3** says, *"(2) And the Lord answered me, and said, write the vision, and make it plain*

> **Your vision statement should be short, precise and to the point.**

upon tables, that he may run that readeth it. (3) For the vision is yet for an appointed time, but at the end it shall speak, and not lie: though it tarry, wait for it; because it will surely come, it will not tarry." The vision must be shared. Andy Stanley, author of *Visioneering* said, "All God-ordained visions are shared visions. Nobody goes it alone. But God generally raises up a point person to paint a compelling verbal picture. A picture that captures the hearts and imaginations of those whom God is calling to embrace the task at hand."

Don't develop long vision statements. It may sound good, but if you cannot put it to memory and place it in your heart, neither can the congregation. Your vision statement should be short, precise and to the point. Our vision statement at Voices of Faith is **"To reach and disciple the unchurched with love and simplicity."**

Use the space below to rewrite your vision statement. Remember, keep it short, precise and to the point:

_____

_____

_____

Once the vision is memorized, one can effectively witness for Jesus Christ. Learn to rid yourself of programs in the church that are not reflecting the vision. The quicker you close ineffective ministries in the church, the quicker you will see results.

Over 70% of the visitors attending our church are invited by our members. It is a good indicator that the vision is in full swing and effectively reaching the unchurched.

Can you think of seven areas in your church where your vision statement could be placed?

Write it down here:

1._____

2._____

3._____

4._____

5._____

6._____

7._____

PURPOSE DRIVEN ONLY!

Purpose driven only should be your church. What is your purpose? Pastors, when you know your purpose, when you know why God has called you to a ministry, you won't allow brush fires to side track you from reaching your destiny. Satan's job is to knock you off course. He does not want you to achieve greatness for God. Dr. I.V. Hilliard, author of *Mental Toughness For Success* said, "There is a price for success which must be paid throughout the life of the pursuit in daily installments, but the most significant part of the price is not the daily installments, but the significant down payment which frightens most people away!"

The founder of McDonald's, the late Ray Kroc, several years ago spoke at a seminar and asked the question, "What business is McDonald's in?" One person raised his hand and said, "McDonald's is in the french fry business." He said, "No." Another said, "McDonald's is in the hamburger business." He said, "No." Another said, "McDonald's is in the fast food business." He said, "No." Ray Kroc said, "McDonald's is in the real estate business." Most McDonalds' are on main highways and busy intersections. Ray Kroc understood his product must be exposed.

I encourage you to write your obituary. Write what you would want people to remember about you. Once you have completed your obituary quit working on assignments that have no or little significance in your life. When you know your purpose, you will focus only on things that matter most.

OLD LEADERS VERSUS NEW LEADERS

Your old leaders will seldom be your new leaders. God will bring people in your ministry to help you at different stages of ministry, but as you go to the next level, God will replace them with new leaders. I am always amazed at the awesomeness of God! Each time a leader leaves for whatever reason, God sends another who is better equipped for the journey. Each time God elevates

> **Each time God elevates your ministry, pruning and purging must take place.**

your ministry, pruning and purging must take place. Don't get upset with leaders who threaten to leave because they no longer are willing to submit to the new vision God has given you. Thank them for their service. That is God's way of pruning for a greater harvest. **Philippians 4:19** says, *"But my God shall supply all your need according to his riches in glory by Christ Jesus."*

SELECTING THE RIGHT BOARD MEMBERS

Selecting board members is one of the most crucial things you will ever have to do in ministry. Never select someone because of friendship and loyalty. There are three things you need to look for when selecting a board member. *First, they must be a Christian.* He or she has to be sold out for Christ. Their desire should be solely to please God. *Second, they must have a submissive spirit.* He or she cannot lead if they are not willing to follow. *Thirdly, they must be business minded.* Many pastors fail in this area. Pastors tend to select board members who have been with the ministry for a long period of time, but they have no vision. You cannot cast a vision with an individual who is accustomed to handling small amounts of money. When God reveals a great vision that will involve millions of dollars, the board member who is not used to handling large amounts of money will vote against the vision. Small thinkers will cripple your vision.

Using these guidelines, list three people in your church who could fit the criteria to be selected as board members:

1._____

2._____

3._____

Deacon Greg Levett, one of my most faithful board members and servants for the Lord continues to push and encourage me to new heights. Recently, I was teaching a church growth seminar and to my amazement Greg Levett was in the audience attending the class. He owns two funeral homes in Atlanta. On this particular day, he was scheduled for several meetings and his company was extremely busy, but he canceled all appointments to support me during the seminar. He is saved, submissive, and an anointed businessman.

SUSTAINING GROWTH
BEYOND YOUR STRUCTURE

You will never sustain growth beyond your structure. If you are structured for 100 people, on a good day, you may pack the house with 150, but you will return to 100 soon after. When your seating capacity is 100, you are not going to continue to increase your membership because folk will not want to come to an overcrowded church.

People like elbow room. Starting a new service will rectify overcrowding.

WHEN TO BEGIN TWO WORSHIP SERVICES?

You should begin a second service when you are out of parking or seats during worship service. Some have suggested when your parking lot is 80 percent full; a new worship service should be implemented. Timing is crucial. The time of year, can make or break your new service times. Spring and Fall are good times to start a new service because of Easter and the beginning of a new school year. Parents are settling back into a routine from vacations. Winter and Summer are bad times to start new worship services due to cold weather and families vacationing.

One of my members said, "Pastor, if we go to two worship services, the sanctuary will not be filled in either one." I told her, "I am not trying to fill every chair; I am trying to reach the needs of the people. The sanctuary will fill up if we reach their needs."

There are people who will never attend your 8:00 a.m. service because they enjoy sleeping late. There are some who will never come to your 11:00 a.m. service because they are early risers. Having two services meets the needs of the people.

THE BENEFITS OF 2 SERVICES ARE GREAT

The benefits of two services are more people serving, more space, double attendance and double your offering. Our 8:00 a.m. worshippers give more in tithe and offering than our 11:00 a.m. worshippers even though more are in attendance at the 11:00 a.m. service.

MATCH PEOPLE'S GIFT TO A MINISTRY

Matching people's gift to ministry is one of the most difficult assignments. Too many people in the body of Christ are not operating in their gifts. Our deacons use to lead our devotion during worship service, but the people were constantly arriving later and later for church. I polled the people to find out how to correct this dilemma. What I discovered was astonishing! Our devotion was killing the people. We had deacons praying, but were not gifted to pray. We had deacons singing, but were not anointed to sing. I immediately removed the deacons from conducting devotion. I

> Too many people in the body of Christ are not operating in their gifts.

replaced them with skilled people who were gifted to pray and anointed to sing. The results were instant success.

Dr. Samuel Chand, Chancellor of Beulah Heights Bible College in Atlanta, Georgia gave this analogy concerning matching people's gifts. There are three important steps to fulfill this task. First, *"Get the right people on the bus."* Make sure the people working in ministry are operating in their gift(s). I believe once an individual finds their calling, they will begin to maximize their fruits. Second, *"Get the wrong people off the bus."* Don't be afraid to remove people who are not operating in their gifts. The quicker this can be achieved the quicker success will take place in your ministry. Finally, *"Get the people on the bus in the right seat."* It is important when matching a person's gift to not just get them on the right bus, but to get them in their right seat. I believe many people are where God wants them to be, however they are working on someone else's assignment. Dr. Chand, who is also the author of the book, *Futuring* said, "The right people in the right place create a winning team."

KEEPING FONT CONSISTENT

Keep your font consistent. This is one of the most common mistakes pastors and churches make when promoting their ministry. Always remain consistent when using fonts with your church's name on it. It creates identity and credibility. Your font will create an identity in itself. For example, Coca Cola uses the same font when advertising. Whether it's sponsoring a sporting event, commercial, or concert, Coca Cola's logo remains the same. Their logo has become the company's identity.

The font Voices of Faith uses to promote the ministry is "New Times Romans." We use it on the church's letterhead, website, television broadcast, marquee, billboards and many other media outlets. I've witnessed many churches changing their font on each new advertisement. It creates confusion and it suggests to potential members unstableness.

Make sure the font you select is easily readable. Remember you are not trying to impress people with beautiful letters, but you are trying to win them to Jesus Christ.

PICK YOUR BATTLES

One of the things pastors have not mastered is learning how to pick their battles. We spend too much time putting out brush fires. Brush fires are small fights and disagreements among the believers that can escalate into a wildfire. Some brush fires are not worth putting out. Every time you slow down to put out a brush fire, it delays you from reaching your destiny. You can't win all of them. Paul demonstrated this in **Acts 16:16-34**. Paul and Silas entered a city where a soothsayer was practicing witchcraft. She

> **Never use God's pulpit to air out dirty laundry.**

recognized Paul and Silas as men of God. She followed them for many days, but Paul ignored her. Finally, after many days of vexing Paul's spirit, he cast the demon out of her. Notice, Paul only responded after many days. She was not his assignment. Brush fires will slow you down. More people will leave your church from brush fires than for any other reason.

Never use God's pulpit to air dirty laundry. God's pulpit is holy. God's pulpit is designed only to teach and preach His Word. I have witnessed too many preachers airing their problems and concerns about others in the pulpit.

NEVER MAKE SPIRITUAL DECISIONS ON FINANCE

Never make spiritual decisions based on your finances. God does not need money to bring about a miracle, He just needs our faith. Money follows faith. Dr. Samuel Chand suggests we ask ourselves four questions when making a spiritual decision for the church. First, *"Is this in line with our vision, mission or core val-*

> **There will be people that will challenge your vision.**

ues?" I have discovered too many pastors are making decisions on major projects and programs that have nothing to do with their vision. Our vision is "to reach and disciple the unchurched with love and simplicity." One of the things we are doing to achieve our vision is broadcasting on television all over the United States. If you don't know where you are going, any road will get you there. <u>Second</u>, *"Do we have the heart for this?"* There will be people that will challenge your vision. They will criticize your decision-making, and they may even leave the church. Knowing what God called you to do is a must. Do you have the heart for the difficult task ahead? <u>Third</u>, *"How will God be glorified?"* If I do this task, how will God get glory? If you are working on a project where God is not getting the glory, stop it immediately! Only what we do for Christ will last. <u>Finally</u>, *"How much will it cost?"* Money should be your last concern. If you can honestly answer the first question, God will send you the money to complete the task at hand. Too many pastors weigh money as the primary concern before embarking on their vision. Remember money follows faith.

PRACTICAL AND RELEVANT MESSAGES

Many of us fail in this area of ministry. We are preaching messages that are not relating to the need of the people. Our messages should be practical and relevant to the daily life of the believer. Preaching about Daniel and the Lion's den and the three Hebrew boys, Shadrach, Meshach, and Abednego, is meaningless if we cannot apply the story to the daily lives of the people. What does preaching about the valley of dry bones have to do with someone's spouse having an affair? What does preaching about

Jesus walking on water have to do with me losing my job? We must be practical and relevant if we are going to reach God's hurting sheep.

Recently, I preached a three part series on harvest time. I dealt with their needs. Our country is in one of the worst recessions in history. Millions have lost jobs, life and health insurance, houses, cars, and personal items. My first message was "Plowing for a Breakthrough" which dealt with praise. Praise loosens up the dirt for your seed to germinate. The next sermon was "Cultivating Your Seed." which spoke of turning over the soil and planting during a drought. A farmer doesn't plant at harvest time, he plants during the spring. It's in the winter months that he cultivates the dirt. The harvest comes during summer. The last message dealt with "The True Vine." This message portrays Jesus as the True Vine and us as the branches. As long as we are connected to Jesus, our lives will yield its maximum fruit. After the three week series, 150 people joined our ministry. I preached where they were hurting.

What are some recent messages you preached that are relevant and practical? Write down three here:

1._____

2._____

3._____

THINK BIG

Growing a great church for God is a mindset. We often think at the level of our ministry. Eleven years ago, we started Voices of Faith with only ten people, but I operated the church as if we were a mega ministry. Even though we were small in numbers, I never thought small. I was always about my Father's business of growing a great church for Him. I was not trying to please man, but my aim was to be in the right relationship with God.

In the beginning of our ministry, we would only have 10 to 15 people show up each Sunday for worship. I would set up over 100 chairs even though a handful was attending. My brother, Aaron asked, "Why do you continue to set up all these chairs when you know only a handful of people will show?" My response, "The chairs I am setting up are not for the people who are coming today, but for the people I believe God will send tomorrow." I never thought with a small mindset. I always thought big!

We must be purpose-driven to grow God's church. We must have a strategy and goals to know whether you have achieved what you set out to accomplish. Dr. John Maxwell, author of *Developing The Leaders Around You* said, "People need clear objectives set before them if they are to achieve anything of value. Success never comes instantaneously. It comes from taking many small steps. A set of goals becomes a map a potential leader can follow in order to grow."

I remember when the total size of our membership was 30. We had only a small amount of money in the bank. I remember driving down a busy highway noticing 20 acres of land. The Holy Spirit instructed me to make a u-turn and pray on the property. I believed God for the land. I contacted the owner of the property and he offered to sell the land for $300,000. The building we designed was going to cost us $450,000. I needed a loan for $750,000. I knew the bank would want a large down payment and at least three strong years of financial stability. We had recently lost over 200 members who had abandoned the ministry. Yet 30 people, of whom 15 were adults remained. I believed God for the land. I did not know how God was going to bless us, I just knew He would. My Minister of Finance, Mia Hawkins, who also is my sister-n-love, put together a business plan to take to the banks for a loan needed to purchase the property. After visiting several banks, one loan officer said, "I have never seen a more professional business plan for a church in 20 years of banking." An accountant, who audited our books said, "This is my very first church audit in 17 years where every "T" was crossed and every "I" was dotted right down to the penny." Needless to say, a few weeks later, a bank gave us the loan to purchase the property because we operated in a spirit of excellence. We never looked at ourselves as small. We always acted like more than conquerors. **Proverbs 23:7** says, *"For as he thinketh in his heart, so is he..."* Thinking big pays great dividends!

Think of some things in your ministry that are impossible to accomplish alone. List seven things you desire that only God can provide. Pursue them as if your life depended on it. Write them here:

1._____

2._____

3._____

4._____

5._____

6._____

7._____

CHAPTER 3

FOR DISCUSSION

1. Why is it important to place your vision statement on everything? Explain.

2. List five areas in your church to place your vision statement.
   1. _____
   2. _____
   3. _____
   4. _____
   5. _____

3. Why will your old leaders seldom be your new leaders as your ministry continue to grow and expand?

4. Do you feel selecting the right board members for your church is critical? Explain.

5. When should you start a second service? What are the benefits?

6. What are the four questions on Spiritual Decisions for the church?

7. Is it important to have a practical and relevant message in the 21st century?

8. What will happen to your church when your vision becomes bigger than your finances?

CHAPTER 4

CREATING A HEALTHY CHURCH

ELIMINATE WASTEFULNESS DURING WORSHIP

Creating a healthy church should be your primary goal. Eliminating wastefulness during worship service is a great place to start. There is too much fat in the worship service that has nothing to do with God. The announcements are too long. It zaps the spirit in the church. Place the information on a bulletin and

Make the visitors remember their visit for a life time.

let them read it. Long drawn out announcements stop the anointing from flowing throughout the service.

Start worship service on time. If it is only one person in the sanctuary, start on time. Keep your word! The people must be trained to arrive on time to worship God. Don't keep the people more than two hours in service. Let them leave enjoying an experience, not tired from a fight.

Keep tithes and offering to a minimum of ten minutes or less. We take up tithes and offering in less than five minutes. We achieve this by passing the offering basket around and not having the congregation march around. Take up one offering. Money is a sensitive subject in the church. There should be no down time during worship.

Serving communion should be done in less than 20 minutes. This can be accomplished by purchasing the "All in one cup." This cup contains both the bread and drink. The communion cup is also disposable.

What are some wasteful things in your church you can eliminate to grow a healthy church?

Write them down here:

1._____

2._____

3._____

4._____

5._____

SETTING THE RIGHT ATMOSPHERE

Setting the right atmosphere for worship is critical for church growth. It starts with the parking ministry. It is very important to choose the right parking attendants for your church. Parking attendants are the first people visitors see upon arriving on your campus. They truly set the atmosphere for worship. Our Parking Ambassadors Ministry is remarkable! They change flat tires during worship service. They fix alternators and change batteries. They park ladies cars during the rain. They bring their bibles to minister to others and upon arriving on campus, each member and visitor gets a hug.

The greeters are also very critical to setting the atmosphere for worship. They greet you with a smile, they remember your name, and each member and visitor gets a hug. Make sure to select the right people in your greeters' ministry who can relate to people. I am amazed to see how many churches have people working in the greeters' ministry without any people skills and with bad attitudes. It truly runs the visitors away.

The Gatekeepers Ministry (ushers) is another important ministry that sets the atmosphere for worship. They escort you to your seat in a very warm and friendly way. They are attentive and alert. The gatekeepers give each visitor a free audio tape of a previous week's message from the pastor. This has been truly successful. It has been one of the most powerful marketing tools at Voices of Faith. It doesn't cost much to buy a thirty-two cent audio tape that the church sells for five dollars. It gives them an opportunity to listen to the audio tape in the comfort of their own car.

Make the visitors remember their first visit for a life time. Try to be the friendliest church in town. You may not be the best preacher. You may not have the best choir in town. Your church may not be as breath taking as others, but you can pride yourself and church as being the friendliest in town. They may choose your church over many others. Make them glad they did. Thom Rainer, author of *Effective Evangelistic Churches* said, "More than any programmatic attempt to start community ministries in a church, the most effective ministries are those that develop from an atmosphere of love and concern."

Can you think of areas in your ministry that will set the atmosphere for worship?

Write them down here:

1._____

2._____

3._____

4._____

5._____

CALL ALL VISITORS YOURSELF

Pastors, this may be the granddaddy of them all! Calling all the visitors yourself each week is the most effective marketing tool. Don't delegate this task to anyone. Many have joined our ministry because I took the time to call. Keep the conversation three minutes or less. Always acknowledge the man of the house. Often

> **My purpose is to lead people to have a greater experience with Christ.**

times a visitor is blown away to hear from the pastor. They may not be surprised by someone else in the church calling or writing a letter, but it blows their mind when it's the pastor. Don't ever feel calling visitors is beneath you. It is easy for me to make the call because I know my purpose. My purpose is to lead people to have a greater experience with Christ. It is truly to get folk saved.

I get angry when very few people join our church. Often times I cannot sleep at night. I feel I have failed God. We average 30 new members a Sunday. A friend of mine, Shon Cooks, often calls after church asking how many joined today. I might say God blessed us with 35 new members. He would be so impressed, but he would detect sadness in my voice. He would say, "There are some churches that don't get 35 new members the entire year and you are upset because God only blessed you with 35." I let him know how grateful I am to God for sending 35 new members, but I knew in my heart there were many others that did not commit their lives to Christ. My purpose is to get folks saved. I'm not preaching for my health. I'm not preaching for myself. I'm preaching because God anointed me to get people saved. It bothers me when only a handful of people join church when I know the world is full of unchurched people. I go back praying asking God to give me a better understanding of how to reach His people. When I come to the podium to preach, I expect people to come down and give their lives to Jesus Christ. I expect it to happen. When I went to Jackson, Mississippi and preached at my good friend's church, Pastor Dwayne Pickett, 50 people gave their lives to Christ during the three day revival. I expected it. I am not being arrogant. I know God anointed me to lead His lost sheep to Christ.

CHAPTER 4

FOR DISCUSSION

1. Why is it important to create a healthy church? Explain.

2. Name five areas during the worship service that can be cut or reduced?
    1. _____
    2. _____
    3. _____
    4. _____
    5. _____

3. Why is it important to keep tithes and offering and announcements to five minutes or less minimum?

4. How can I serve communion in my church in less than 20 minutes?

5. Do you feel setting the atmosphere is critical for church growth?

6. List five areas in the church that would set the atmosphere.
    1. _____
    2. _____
    3. _____
    4. _____
    5. _____

7. What role the gatekeeper plays in setting the atmosphere?

8. Why is it critically important for the pastor to call all of the visitors?

CHAPTER 5

ME TIME!

This is an area where over 75% of pastors lack, causing mental breakdowns and burnout. We are so busy pursuing ministry and setting goals for ourselves and our ministries that we have placed very little time for family, exercise and "me time." We are so focused on going after our destiny, yet our bodies are yelling, "fatigue!" "Me Time" is what I call taking time to pamper ones self. "Me Time" is when pastors take the time to wine and dine themselves. Pastors are oftentimes ministering to other people's needs, yet their health and home life are suffering. I am constantly hearing horror stories of pastors quitting ministry everyday because of burnout and fatigue. Pastors, if you are going to take your cities

> **Pastors, a critical area of concern has to be our health.**

for the kingdom of God, there must be a balance in your life. We must take the time and find things that we enjoy doing. Pastors, if you have not heard, stress will kill you.

I am an avid movie goer. I love going to the movies. I love great westerns, action, comedy, and drama movies. I don't care for horror movies. At least once a week, my family and I attend a movie. Movies relax me. Whenever I feel extremely stressed about something, I take the time to attend a movie. On special occasions, I may leave the office and catch a mid-afternoon movie. We built a home theater in our basement so that our family could enjoy watching a movie in the comfort of our home. It has been one of our greatest investments. Once a week, my family watches a movie in our home theater. Sometimes all of the kids pile in bed with Debbie and me to watch a movie when we don't feel like going to the home theater in the basement. Popcorn and fruit juices are a must at the movies. There is such peace that falls over me when I am enjoying a movie with my family.

Pastors, movies may not be your cup of tea. You may enjoy golfing. There are so many pastors who are avid golfers. I have been told on many occasions that once you start golfing, you are hooked for life. For some, reading a great book or fishing may be your idea of relaxation. There is serenity on the still waters waiting for fish to bite. For others it might be playing tennis or playing a pickup game of basketball. Playing the popular video games such as Xbox and Playstation II will relax many people.

Whatever relaxes you away from the church is what I prescribe for you.

My boys, Gary Jr. and Kalen and I are great sports fans. I am a season ticket holder with the Atlanta Hawks. We have great seats for four on the floor at mid-court. The fours seats usually include: Debbie, Gary Jr., Kalen, and myself. My daughters, Elaina and Ashley often use the tickets with their friends when I have scheduled conflicts. My daughters are twenty-one and nineteen years of age. As they have gotten older, it's hard to slow them down for family time. They enjoy hanging out with their friends. It is a great time of bonding with my children. They enjoy going to the games watching their favorite players and eating the many assortments of food and snacks that Phillips Arena provides. When we are home and its football season, we are usually watching the Atlanta Falcons football games in the comfort of our family room. We also enjoy watching our favorite college teams, Southern University and Louisiana State University

I am very active in my sons' sports activities as well. Summer of 2005 was amazing! I coached my two sons' basketball team. Debbie was the team mom. Don't ask me how we did it with our hectic schedules but, God provided us with grace and mercy to endure to the end. Debbie and I were running so much with our busy schedules that we felt convicted to spend more quality time with our sons. Our daughters need quality attention as well, but they are off in college and working a full-time job. Coaching my sons' team would provide the quality time I was seeking. It was a twofold blessing for me. First, I got an opportunity to spend quality time with them and to deposit my passion and skills into them. Second, I was a McDonald's High School Basketball All-American in Baton Rouge, Louisiana. I had the opportunity to use my knowledge and skills to help develop and sharpen their skills. We were in the Voices of Faith basketball league. The league was comprised of approximately seven churches. I coached the 9-11 year old. We went undefeated throughout the regular season and won the championship. Praise the Lord! That was a special moment for me. As a matter of fact, I currently have the championship trophy in my office.

Pastors, a critical area of concern has to be our health. We are so busy laying hands on other folks and giving advice to them, yet our bodies are breaking down like a broken record. Don't spend your entire life building a great church for God only to see someone else enjoy the fruits of YOUR labor. Exercise must be a priority in your life.

Five days a week, Debbie and I workout together in our church's Family Life Center weight room. Our average workout last about an hour. We usually workout early in the morning before our day gets started. We have a personal trainer, Yvette "YaYa" Green, who pushes us to the limit. She maximizes our time with her. I have found myself much stronger in the pulpit on Sundays and Wednesdays because of my conditioning. Regular exercise is a good defense against cardiovascular disease. There are so many things you could do that would help you improve your cardiovascular system. Here are a few things the February 2005 issue of Ebony Magazine suggests that will improve your cardiovascular system:

a. Walking is one exercise that can be a family affair.

b. If you ride the train or the bus, get off a few stops before your stop and walk the rest of the way home or to work.

c. Do some form of moderate-intensity exercise for 20 minutes each day, such as dancing, stationary cycling, floor exercises or lifting free-weights.

d. Take the stairs instead of the elevator or escalator.

e. Instead of snacking in front of the television at night, do chores around the house.

f. Have dinner and then go out dancing, bowling or skating.

Pastors, one of the things Debbie and I started doing more of recently was going out enjoying fine dining. My big brother in ministry, Pastor Raymond W. Johnson of Baton Rouge, Louisiana encouraged us to spend more time fine dining with one another. Atlanta is known across America as a city for great restaurants. We were used to stopping at every fast food restaurant eating all the wrong kind of foods which often made us sick. We make it a point each week to enjoy fine dining with each other. It gives us an opportunity to communicate more effectively with less stress.

Another favorite "Me Time" is eating dinner at home immediately after church. Our daily schedules have become so hectic that we do not have adequate time to prepare a meal on Sundays.

Sundays are one of my favorite times to have a home cooked meal. We decided to hire a full-time chef (Collard Alexander) on staff at the church that would provide meals for my family and me every Sunday at our home. Each week we give the chef our preferred menu for Sunday. It has been great! I can not tell you how frustrated it was leaving church after preaching three times on Sunday mornings and then having to wait in line for an hour at a restaurant. Now I can leave church and come straight home and change my clothing into something more comfortable and eat an excellent meal in the comfort of my home. Our chef also provides breakfast and lunch for the staff twice a week. She also helps out with the kitchen ministry on Wednesday nights before and after Mid-week worship service.

Getting massages is a must in ministry! I am guilty of this as well. Massages helps to relax your body and remove unwanted stress. There are some pastors around the country who get massages done on a regular basis. One prominent pastor in the Atlanta area gets a massage three times a week.

A couple of months ago, I was ministering at my spiritual son's, (Pastor Anderson Lewis) church in Little Rock, Arkansas. Upon my arrival, he immediately took me to get a massage. I was somewhat reluctant at first, but I decided to go ahead and have the massage because he went through so much trouble to set it up. Afterwards, I felt like the weight of the world had been lifted off me. It was the best massage I ever had. I felt energized to do ministry in a powerful way. It is "Me Time" now. I will make a commitment to get a massage at least once a month.

When is the last time you had a good laugh? Laughter is good for the soul and oftentimes as pastors, we become so holy until we're no earthly good. Laughter relaxes you and you'll find your members will loosen up and laugh with you

> **Life is too short to put off tomorrow what you can do now.**

not at you. If you don't begin to laugh at life then life will surely laugh at you.

Pastors, work hard, but take the time to enjoy the fruits of your labor. Enjoy family time! Life is too short to put off tomorrow what you can do now. Take the necessary vacations. Trust others to preach a relevant Word in your absence. It is "Me Time." It is time to pamper your self!

CHAPTER 5

FOR DISCUSSION

1. Why is it that over 75 percent of pastors lack "Me Time?" Explain.

2. What is your favorite past time? List five other things you enjoy that relax you.
   1. _____
   2. _____
   3. _____
   4. _____
   5. _____

3. What are some things you enjoy during with your family?

4. When was the last time you enjoyed a massage?

5. When was the last time you treated yourself to a five star restaurant?

6. Do you enjoy fine dining or do you prefer a home cooked meal? Explain.

7. Is it important to have a balance lifestyle? Why or Why not?

8. When was the last time you took a vacation? Where do you go?

CHAPTER 6

THE LAW OF ENVIRONMENT

I believe the Law of Environment may be the most important information you will receive in this book. It is critical that you connect with other pastors, business executives, and leaders who are heading down the same highway as you. I am oftentimes amazed that so many pastors tend to hang around leaders who are in the same shape if not worse. Neither can truly learn from the other. Neither can bring anything fresh and new to the table that will enhance their ministries.

How can I make the Law of Environment work for me?

Both ministries become two peas in a pot. You look like each other, your characteristics are the same, and as a result, both ministries are producing the same kind of fruit.

It is vitality important to associate with pastors and leaders who are already treading in waters you are trying to swim. Your environment will change you before you change it. Your environment is absolutely critical! It will change your lifestyle before you change it. If I hang out with people that are lazy, content, and satisfied with the current status of their ministries, before I change them the Law of Environment says, they would change me to operate with the same kind of mindset. If I am associated with people that use profanity the Law of Environment says, before I stop them from using profanity, I will start using it. How can I make the Law of Environment work for me? I have to be careful of the people with whom I associate. If I hang with a pastor or a leader whose vision is to take their cities for the kingdom of God, before they come to my level of thinking, I would go to their level. I will start speaking that I am going to take my city. Your environment is contagious. It is critical to your success in life. Choosing who you hang around can make or break your ministry.

Association breeds assimilation. You must be willing to be mentored. In March 2000, Voices of Faith Ministries was having its first "Corporate Prayer Conference." We were approximately 200 members strong at the time. Very few people knew who we were. My big spiritual brother, Gregory B. Levett of Levett and Sons Funeral Home is a very close friend to Bishop Eddie L. Long. With his help, we invited Bishop Long to be our featured speaker. Bishop Long pastors a church with over 25,000 members. While ministering, Bishop Long stopped and turned to

Debbie and I and said, "God told me that you are to be my spiritual son and daughter." We immediately received the impartation and transformation. At the time, I had no previous relationship with Bishop Long. The very first time I had ever met him was in my church office minutes before he was to preach the Word of God. The

> **When I changed my environment, I changed the results of our ministry.**

"Corporate Prayer" Conference was held on a Saturday morning. After accepting him as my spiritual covering, it seems as if our ministry made a major leap over night. The very next day, which was a Sunday morning, we had 34 people to join our church. It seemed as if Bishop Long left the residue of the anointing and favor that God had placed on his life. Our ministry has continued to grow at an alarming rate every since. I connected with someone that was much more advanced than our ministry. The anointing and favor that God had placed upon Bishop Long and New Birth was now transformed on ours. The anointing and favor pushed our ministry into another dimension. When I changed my environment, I changed the results of our ministry.

In October 2004, I visited Dr. I.V. Hilliard, pastor of New Light Christian Center Church's "Leadership and Growth" Conference. I was invited by Dr. Hilliard to attend the conference. Dr. Hilliard had ordered my book, "Marketing Your Church For Growth" from our website. I met him at another conference where he was ministering. The conference was phenomenal!

Dr. Hilliard pastors a church with over 22,000 members. He is known for his teachings on faith and finances. In the eleven years of our ministry, I had never taught a series on finances, but connecting with Dr. Hilliard gave me the courage to speak on this subject. In January 2005, I spoke on a four-week sermon on finances. Every Saturday night for an hour during the month of January, Dr. Hilliard walked me through the teachings on tithing, offering, sowing and reaping a harvest. It was one of the most exciting things that had ever happened to me in ministry. I was getting a personal touch from a man of God with proven principles. After two weeks of teaching on finances, I announced to our congregation that we were going to raise money to pay off debt at our church. The first Sunday in February 2005, we raised a total of approximately $600,000. Praise The Lord! This could not have happen if I would have hung out with pastors on my level. I needed to be associated with someone that was already operating in this kind of anointing. Notice, <u>before</u> Bishop Long came down to our level of growth; we were heading upward towards his level of growth. <u>Before</u> Dr. I.V. Hilliard comes down to our level of finances, we are heading upward towards his level of finances.

Don't hang around "visionless" leaders. Associate yourselves with pastors who cast visions that are over their heads. Mingle with pastors who have great faith and believe that the impossible is possible. The people you keep company with will either enhance you or diminish you. **Proverbs 27:17** says, *"Iron* *sharpeneth iron; so a man sharpeneth the countenance of his friend."* Everything in life is relationship. Everything you will ever accomplish or fail to accomplish will be bound up with other people. I have made it a point in my ministry to become a life long learner of the Word of God and to mimic the success stories in other ministries. Too many of us are trying to re-invent the wheel. Our pride often negates the behavior to copy the success from someone else's ministry. Remember, The Law of Environment says, "Your environment will change you before you change it."

BECOMING AN EXPERT IN YOUR FIELD

Every preacher who is at the top 10% of their profession once started at the bottom 10%. Every preacher that is successful today in ministry was once doing poorly. No one is better than you and no one is smarter than you. You must wake up every morning and tell

> **You were born for greatness!**

yourself those encouraging words. You were born for greatness! Your destiny is tied to your affirmation. Listed below are spiritual leaders that have become experts in their field. I believe their anointing rest in these areas:

Peter was known for preaching to the Jews. His ministry only focused on those who were circumcised. In the book of Acts, Peter was somewhat surprised when God summoned him to go to

Cornelius house who was a Gentile and preach the Gospel. He thought salvation was for the Jews only. **Acts 10:34-35** says, *"(34) Then Peter opened his mouth, and said, Of a truth I perceive that God is no respecter of persons. (35) But in every nation he that feareth him, and worketh righteousness, is accepted with him."*

Paul was known for preaching the Gospel to the Gentiles. **Acts 9:15-17** says, *"(15) But the Lord said unto him, Go thy way: for he is a chosen vessel unto me, to bear my name before the Gentiles, and kings, and the children of Israel. (16) For I will show him how great things he must suffer for my name's sake. (17) And Ananias went his way, and entered into the house; and putting his hands on him said, Brother Saul, the Lord, even Jesus, that appeared unto thee in the way as thou camest, hath sent me, that thou mightest receive thy sight, and be filled with the Holy Ghost."* Paul dedicated his life to preaching to the Gentiles. Even though he was a Jew, God gave him an assignment that would get Gentiles saved.

Bishop Eddie L. Long is known for preaching on authority in the kingdom. Over 25,000 people have joined his church because God has anointed Bishop Long to preach about the kingdom of heaven.

Bishop T.D. Jakes of The Potter's House in Dallas, Texas is known for preaching to hurting women. Even though God has gifted him to minister effectively on all subjects in the bible, his anointing is connected with hurting women. "Woman Thou Art

Loosed" Conference is one of the biggest women's conferences in the world. Eighty thousand women come from all over the world to be delivered from depression, sickness, and other things that have stopped their blessings from the Lord. His very anointing from the Lord is with hurting women.

Joel Osteen of Lakewood Church in Houston, Texas is known for preaching to the simple man an encouraging message. His messages are often so simple that a child can understand. Joel Osteen simplistic approach to ministry has brought over 30,000 people to his church on Sunday mornings. Lakewood is now the largest church in North America.

Benny Hinn is known for ministering on healing. One cannot even think about Benny Hinn and not associate healing with his name. He travels the globe and put on crusades to jam-packed arenas and coliseums. People don't show up to a Benny Hinn conference to hear him preach even though he is an accomplish speaker. They come because they believe God has placed a healing anointing on his life.

Prophetess Juanita Bynum is known for preaching on deliverance. Almost every sermon she preaches, someone will get delivered from something. Joyce Meyers is known for preaching on righteous living. Dr. I.V. Hilliard is known for preaching on Faith. Dr. Creflo Dollar of World Changers Ministries in College Park, Georgia is known for preaching and teaching on prosperity. Dr. William Sheals of Hopewell Baptist Church in Norcross, Georgia is known for preaching on Salvation. This is just to name a few.

I believe the moment you find your anointing; your ministry will take on a dimension that will elevate you to a level that is beyond your understanding. My anointing is on faith. The moment I discovered my anointing, my ministry exploded on the scene. Whenever I minister on subjects dealing with faith, 50 to over 100 people join our church per Sunday. Is this by coincidence?

When you discover your anointing, you will become an expert in your field.

No, I have tapped into an anointing that God has given to me to grow a great church. The great thing about the anointing is you do not have to copy from someone's preaching or teaching. God gives each of us gifts that will bless the body of Christ. **Matthew 25:14-15** says, *"(14) For the kingdom of heaven is as a man travelling into a far country, who called his own servants, and delivered unto them his goods. (15) And unto one he gave five talents, to another two, and to another one; to every man according to his several ability; and straightway took his journey."* God blessed you with tremendous gifts the moment He saw your abilities. You must pray and ask God to reveal to you your assignment and where the anointing rest on your life. When you discover your anointing, you will become an expert in your field.

CHAPTER 6

FOR DISCUSSION

1. What is the definition of "The Law of Environment"?

2. Why is it important to associate with pastors and leaders who are already where you are trying to go?

3. Name at least seven people that you admire in ministry and desire to go where God has blessed them.
   1. _____
   2. _____
   3. _____
   4. _____
   5. _____
   6. _____
   7. _____

4. How can I make the Law of Environment work for me?

5. How do I become an expert in my field?

6. What popular minister is known for preaching on authority?

7. What preacher is known for preaching to hurting women?

8. Who in the body of Christ is known for teaching on healing?

CHAPTER 7

FOUR GODLY PRINCIPLES
OF MENTAL IMAGE

Godly principles are extremely powerful and anointed. Even if you are unaware you are operating the Godly principles, they will still work for you. For many years, I grew my church on the principles of God, yet not knowing I was already operating under the anointing. God's principles are no respecter of a person. I believe the four principles of mental image taught in this chapter will change your ministry and elevate the anointing upon you to manifest the harvest that God intended for your life.

PRINCIPLE ONE:
HOW OFTEN DO YOU THINK
OF THE BLESSING?

Principle one tells God whether or not you are serious about doing His business for the kingdom. It exposes your character and integrity for the Lord. If you desire God to do something incredible in your life, your mind will think of nothing else but the subject matter at hand. Every blessing I have ever received as a pastor has come from using this principle. Once I get my mind fixed on something I can not think of anything else until God accomplishes it. How often do you think of the blessing? The blessing must be on your mind 24 hours a day and 7 days a week. Sometimes focusing that much attention on a subject matter can weaken and cause fatigue to your body. It can even cause sickness to your body if you are not getting the proper rest. I used this very principle in May-July, 2004 until it made me physically sick.

> **The blessing must be on your mind 24 hours a day and 7 days a week.**

In May 2004, I heard clearly from God to start a new church in Conyers, Georgia which is located in Rockdale County. I even heard God speak to me about the start date. It was July 18, 2004. I broke the news to our congregation and they were excited with the vision God gave to me. I had nothing else on my mind but to find a place to worship for our 9:30 a.m. Sunday morning worship service. I rose early every morning with excitement on my mind. I was on an assignment and I was determined to see it through. Every day for hours at a time I drove around Conyers looking for land, a school, recreation center, and/or a store front to hold our worship service. I was filling my gas tank up sometimes twice a day. I talked with owners of shopping centers about renting their facilities, but their rent was too high and their leases were too long. I had no desire to spend five years tied to a lease in a shopping center. I started visiting local schools in the area. I visited elementary, middle, and high schools. They all told me that I had to get approval from the Rockdale County Board of Directors. I went to visit the Superintendent of Rockdale County School System. He turned me down. He explained that our church did not fit the criteria for using the local schools. The Rockdale County School Board rule states that you must own property in the county before you are allowed to utilize their facilities. We did not own any property in Rockdale County. I was determined to find a way to get in the county to do ministry for the kingdom. Time was ticking and July 18 was quickly approaching. I visited several local recreation centers and to my surprise, they too were connected to the same system as the Rockdale County School Board. I visited the local government in the city of Conyers where several churches were vacant and being use for government work. Once again, I was turned down because they were also connected to the same system as the

Rockdale County School Board. I had never experienced a county on one accord such as Rockdale County. I had no where to turn and time was running out. I decided to visit churches in the area. I asked several pastors and churches could I utilize their facilities at 9:30 a.m. on Sunday mornings and they all said no. It was understandable. Most Sunday mornings across America at 9:30 a.m. is Sunday School hour. I had nothing else on my mind, but Rockdale County and Conyers, Georgia. I became fatigued and physically sick. I went home and stayed in the bed for two days. On the second day of sulking and complaining, God told me to get up out of bed and go back again and have a meeting with the same superintendent who turned me down. I told the superintendent that I had 14 days left before July 18th and I must worship in Rockdale County on that day. I was on a mission from God and there was no turning around. The superintendent asked me to attend the weekly Board of Directors meeting, which was held every Thursday. If a rule could be broken, it would occur there. I showed up with boldness, like any desperate man who has heard from the Lord. When they got to my name, they asked me to stand and state the cause of my presence. I shared with them my heart and vision for the county and that on July 18th I MUST start our first worship service in Rockdale County. They said, "Pastor Hawkins, no one has ever challenged our ruling until now. Give us a week to discuss the matter further." I was desperate. I had 10 days before the opening of our new church. I could not wait until I heard from the Board of Directors. I announced to my leaders to make a brochure and pass out 5,000 fliers throughout Conyers and Rockdale County. Even though the Board of Directors had not yet voted, I told the people of Rockdale County that we would hold our very first worship service at Rockdale County High School. When I arrived at the meeting the next week, the Board of Directors asked me to stand. They said, "Pastor Hawkins, didn't we ask you to wait until next week before you told people in the county that you would use our facilities? Since you have already passed out fliers telling the people of Rockdale County that you will have your very first church service at Rockdale County High School, we will grant you permission to use the facility for two weeks and afterwards you will move your church service to Conyers Middle School." Praise the Lord!

The more I saw myself worshipping in Conyers, the more the mental picture in my mind became a reality. I saw our church; then I pursued it to manifest the harvest that God spoke about. How often do you think of the blessing? God is testing you. He wants to know how bad do you want the blessing.

PRINCIPLE TWO:
HOW LONG DO YOU THINK
OF THE BLESSING?

Principle two is closely related to fasting. This principle separates the hearers from the doers of the Word of God. If you have

We are all over the place in our prayer lives.

something on your mind that you desire God to do, it will not leave you until God blesses it. I believe our prayer life suffers from this very thing. We are all over the place in our prayers. One moment we are asking God to bless us with a spouse. The next moment we are praying for a new house. The following prayer request, we petition God for a promotion on our jobs. We are all over the place in our prayer life. We don't stay still long enough to see the hand of God at work in our lives.

I am reminded of the disciples' lack of faith, prayer, and fasting in the book of Matthew. A father brings his son to the disciples to heal him. The son was a lunatic, he oftentimes throws himself into the fire and water. In Matthew the disciples were unable to heal him. After Jesus heals the boy His disciples approach Jesus and asked, "Why could not we cast him out?" Notice Jesus answer. In **Matthew 17:21** Jesus said, *"Howbeit this kind goeth not out but by prayer and fasting."* In other words, Jesus said the greater the blessing, the greater the concentration. Jesus was teaching us that the longer we can focus on a subject matter, our chances increase for a blessing. You must use all of your energy level for an extended period of time and focus only on the one blessing you desire from the Lord. **Philippians 3:13-14** says, *"(13) Brethren, I count not myself to have apprehended: but this one thing I do, forgetting those things which are behind, and reaching forth unto those things which are before, (14) I press toward the mark for the prize of the high calling of God in Christ Jesus."* I forget the ground I have covered in the race and the people that have offended me during the course. I only reach for the one thing that is before me in the race. We are running in a race for our lives. I strain every nerve and muscle and exhaust every ounce of strength to win. Yes, I mean to win. You are not in the race to compete, but to win. My future depends on my desperateness. My wife and children are connected to my ability to win. I am running for my life. I press toward the mark, that is, I pursue the tape at the finish line which all runners must keep their eyes fixed.

Fasting is the key to holding a mental picture in your mind. Fasting forces you to concentrate on your blessing. Fasting teaches you how to focus on the blessing. The world fasts for various reasons, but God designed fasting for concentration and purification. Fasting helps to cleanse the body.

> **Fasting is the key to holding a mental picture in your mind.**

The longer you can hold a mental picture, the more deeply it will be impressed into your subconscious. The moment something gets in my mind, I start having dreams about the subject matter. I find myself daydreaming about the blessing. If I rolled over in my bed at 3:00 a.m. I find myself thinking about the blessing. My mind has pushed all the insignificant things out of it and has only channeled all energy on the very thing I desire from the Lord.

I believe this may be the most difficult principle because it requires us to wait upon the Lord. Our manifestation does not come over night. Many of us don't have the stamina and staying power to wait on the Lord. When God does not move on our time schedule, we began to go ahead of the Lord. The trials we experience in life are preparing us for a greater harvest from the Lord. Our trials and setbacks teach us patience. **Romans 5:3-4** says, *"(3) And not only so, but we glory in tribulations also: knowing that tribulation worketh patience; (4) And patience, experience; and experience, hope."* Waiting for our breakthrough to come builds our character.

PRINCIPLE THREE:
HOW CLEARLY CAN YOU SEE THE BLESSING?

In principle three, it deals with the ability to see the blessing before the manifestation. For many pastors and leaders, that is a difficult thing to do. We will not trust the Lord until we can physically touch or feel the blessing. **Hebrews 11:1** says, *"Now faith is the substance of things hoped for, the evidence of things not seen."* I have to develop the ability to see it, claim it, and possess it even though I don't physically have it.

The very first building we ever built at Voices of Faith Ministries was a 6,000-square-feet sanctuary in July 1999. The sanctuary seats 400. Long before our church was built I saw what it would look like. I saw the color of the church. I saw which bricks I would use. I saw the trim work. I saw the color of the inside sanctuary. I saw the seats we would purchase. I saw the dimension and square-footage. I would take pastors on the site and show them exactly where the building would sit. Even though there was no foundation, I saw it before God built it. I drew the plans in my home office. I pictured myself worshipping in the building. I saw myself working in my office. I saw people entering the parking lot from the east, west, north, and south. It is not by coincidence that God has grown our ministry as fast as He has. I saw the people in large numbers come to our church before it happened.

Earlier I shared with you, when we worshipped at the Brownsmill Recreation Center, I would tell my brother, Aaron to put 100 chairs out each Sunday. Remember, we only had ten people showing up and they were my children, nieces and nephews. It truly was a family affair. After many weeks of doing this, he questioned my decision. Aaron said, "Why do we continue to put 100 chairs out each Sunday when only ten people will show up?" I said, "These chairs are not for the ones who are currently here, but for the ones God showed me was coming." I saw vividly in my mind that we would not be able to hold the people God was sending our direction. The vision stayed before me.

Once the church was built, we quickly ran out of space. We immediately went to two services. Within six months, the two services had reached capacity. We opened up a third service and five months later was completely full. We opened up and converted two buildings next to us for over flow. One and a half years later of being in our new sanctuary, we had to start working on plans for our Family Life Center that seats 2,300. God manifested what I first saw clearly in my mind and spirit. The vividness of your desire directly determines how quickly it materializes in the world around you.

The more vivid the picture shows up in my mind, the quicker the manifestation. Writing the blessing down helps you to see what the blessing would look like. **Habakkuk 2:2-3** says, *"(2) And the LORD answered me, and said, Write the vision, and make it plain upon tables, that he may run that readeth it. (3) For the vision is yet for an appointed time, but at the end it shall speak, and not lie: though it tarry, wait for it; because it will surely come, it will not tarry."* In order for a blessing to come to pass, you must breath, eat, and live your heart's desire. I find myself thinking of the blessing so much that the slightest thing people do reminds me of what I am waiting for God to manifest. The moment you can clearly see the blessing is the very moment God start to fulfill it for you.

PRINCIPLE FOUR:
HOW INTENSELY CAN YOU
FEEL THE BLESSING?

In principle four, it deals with the ability to not except "no" for an answer. Principle four teaches us how to develop a stubborn will that will not go away. This principle requires great faith. You must prepare yourself for the battlefield. There may be some scars, cuts, and bruises when you come out of this spiritual warfare, but in the end God will get the glory. This principle also focuses on our emotions. At this level, we

> **We must rid ourselves of negative people that may discourage us in our walk with the Lord.**

must stay before the Lord until He answers. We must trust Him with our whole heart even though it does not seem anything is happening. We must rid ourselves of negative people that may discourage us in our walk with the Lord.

Psalms 1:2 says, *"But his delight is in the law of the LORD; and in his law doth he meditate day and night."* Our passion and desire for the blessing that you are requesting from the Lord must be so intense that you can reach out and touch it. This principle requires a different kind of mindset. It requires a different kind of faith. You must take God at His Word and respond. I am reminded of the centurion in the book of Matthew who had a soldier who was sick with palsy and terribly ill. He asked Jesus to speak the

Word only and his soldier would be healed. Jesus was amazed at the level of his faith. **Matthew 8:10** says, *"When Jesus heard it, he marveled, and said to them that followed, Verily I say unto you, I have not found so great faith, no not in Israel."* The centurion expressed absolute faith in the power of Jesus Christ. The centurion had power and authority over 100 men who obeyed him the moment he spoke. He recognized that Jesus possessed greater power than he. The centurion recognized Jesus had authority over demons and one Word from Him would be enough to heal his servant. What faith! This is the different kind of faith we must possess to please the Lord.

The Law of Super-Conscious Activity says, "Any thought, plan, goal, or idea held continuously in the conscious mind must inevitably be brought into reality by the super conscious." In other words, whatever you intensely place on your mind for an extended period of time will be manifested in the flesh. I know this principle works.

In 1989, I began to experience dreams of preaching in the pulpit. Even though I could not even speak before a small group, God was allowing me to dream dreams of preaching the Word of the Lord before a large body of believers. This blows me away because I had no desire to become a preacher. As a matter of fact, I ran from the calling for years. But the dreams became more and more frequent. I remember one week in 1989 where the dreams intensified. I kept dreaming I was preaching before a large body of believers. I dreamed I approached the pulpit and said, "There is a Word" but I would shake myself to wake myself up because I had no desire to preach the Word of the Lord. This happened almost every night for a week, but the last dream was different. I dreamed I approached the pulpit as usual and said, "There is a Word and the Word can be found in Matthew 22:14." God would not let me shake myself and wake up like before. But this time after telling the congregation to turn to Matthew 22:14 God wakes me up. I immediately jumped out of bed to find my bible. I said, "God why didn't you allow me to read the scripture?" God responded by saying, "It is time to grab the mantle and preach my Word so that thousands may be saved." I opened up my bible and found **Matthew 22:14**, *"For many are called, but few are chosen."* I immediately recognized that I was personally chosen by God. Now whenever I preach the Word of the Lord, I always say to the congregation what I saw in my dreams, "There is a Word and the Word can be found in..." Every time I say those words, God is manifesting what I saw in my dreams. How intensely can you feel the blessing?

If you follow these four principles found in this chapter your ministry will leapfrog to the next level. Remember, you can not be just a hearer of these words, but in order for your ministry to change and grow, you must be a doer of the Word of the Lord.

CHAPTER 7

FOR DISCUSSION

1. What are the four Godly principles of mental image?
   1. _____
   2. _____
   3. _____
   4. _____

2. How often do you think of the blessing? Explain.

3. How long do you think of the blessing? Explain.

4. How clearly do you see the blessing? Explain.

5. How intensely can you feel the blessing? Explain.

6. What is the definition of "The Law of Super-Conscious Activity"?

7. What causes the mental picture in your mind to become reality?

8. How difficult is it to see the blessing before the manifestation?

CHAPTER 8

THIS AND THAT

I want to spend time in my final chapter talking with you about various things I feel that will grow and mature your church.

PERSIST UNTIL YOU SUCCEED.

Fear is, and always has been the greatest enemy of mankind. Fear has defeated many Christians over the years. Fear has kept the overflow blessing from God away from our lives. In **2 Timothy** 1:7 it says, *"For God hath not given us the spirit of fear; but of power, and of love, and of a sound mind."* The moment we began to walk in the newest of the Lord and His boldness, a fresh anointing will fall upon our lives.

Fear is caused by ignorance.

Courage can be learned, but you must work to conquer your fear. I have discovered the more Word I receive, the stronger my faith becomes. **Romans 10:17** says, *"So then faith cometh by hearing, and hearing by the word of God."* My motto is to feed *my faith and starve my doubts."* In other words, I only put positive affirmation in my mind. I don't allow negative people to enter my spirit.

Fear is caused by ignorance. When we have limited information we become tense and insecure. Before we pursue a task, do your homework. Oftentimes, you will discover the problem is not as big as it seems. Fear comes from a lack of knowledge. **Proverbs 4:7** says, *"Wisdom is the principal thing; therefore get wisdom: and with all thy getting get understanding."* Fatigue is a major factor of fear. When I am tired, it is difficult for me to concentrate. Getting the proper rest will help your mind to function.

Everyone is afraid. Mark Twain said, "Courage is resistance to fear, mastery of fear—-not absence of fear." There is not one project I ever pursued that I was not afraid. I refuse to allow fear to paralyze me. Don't be afraid to fail. Disappointment is inevitable. If God allows me to pastor long enough, mistakes will occur.

In this day in time, faith rules! **Hebrews 11:6** says, *"But without faith it is impossible to please him: for he that cometh to God must believe that he is, and that he is a rewarder of them that diligently seek him."* The future belongs to risk takers. God is waiting on you to step out on faith so that He can bless you.

Remember, fear and failure are steps of life that gets us to the blessings of God.

THE TRINITY RULE.

The trinity rule is a very simplistic rule I use to better understand "Church Folk." The trinity rule helps you to understand the condition of your church. The trinity rule says if 100 people joined your church:

A. The first third will become extremely active and faithful. The first 33 are your committed members. They will support your vision. They will participate in most of your activities. They will support the ministry with their tithes and offering.

B. The second third are off and on Christians. They are lukewarm. They are neither hot nor cold. They will show up to church twice a month. The second third might participate in an activity at the church or they might not. More than likely they don't pay tithes.

C. The last third are seasonal Christians. You will only see them on special occasions. They are more likely to show up on Christmas, Mother's Day, and Easter. You can not grow your church with this group.

Every church in America faces these same criteria. It does not matter what size your ministry. It does not matter what ethnic group. It does not matter whether your ministry is located in the south, north, east or west. Church people are the same all over America.

World re-known ministries face these issues as well. There are some mega-churches across America with over 20,000 members, but their sanctuary may hold 7,000 seats. They only have two services. If given the benefit of the doubt, say both services are full, where are the other 6,000?

What can be done about this? No matter what you do, you can not stop the back door. The back door is impossible to stop. It has nothing to do with the preacher. It is a sin problem. There are some people who walk down the isles and join your church; you will never see them again on this side of glory. People are not committed to the Lord.

You must recruit the front door. You must continue to market your church and share the Gospel with them. You are going to lose people no matter how talented you may be in the pulpit. People are going to leave. Quit spending 80% of your time chasing the people who are leaving your ministry. Focus your attention on the church members who have made a commitment to stay.

Several years ago, we had 250 members at the church. I told the church, God called me to go full time in ministry. Some deacons and ministers did not want to see me go full time. They called all of the members up and had a private meeting to vote against the Lord's will for my life. Well, 220 people left the church. It destroyed my family, but we decided to trust the Lord.

We had 30 members who stayed. I only focused on the ones who stayed. I preached as if nothing had happened even though I was hurting on the inside. One of the members approached me a few weeks later and said, "Pastor Hawkins, the reason my family never left because you never criticized anyone from your pulpit. You only focused on the ones who stayed." It was a life changing experience. God taught me to totally trust His Word.

THE LAW OF THE HARVEST.

God desires to bless our lives, but He placed a systematic process that we must follow in order to get the blessing. I want to use the process of a farmer to use as my analogy. A farmer works tirelessly to produce quality crops. He understands that if he is going to be successful, he can not take short cuts. Too many pastors and leaders try to take short cuts to success. It does not happen. You must pay the price with hard work, integrity, and good character. Everything happens through hard work preparation, perseverance, and patience. A lazy farmer can not grow a good crop. A lazy pastor can not grow a great church for the kingdom. He must be progressive.

> There is no such thing as an overnight success.

Preparing the ground takes time. The soil must be worked over time in order to produce a harvest. Nothing happens over night. There is no such thing as an overnight success. Success is hard work. A farmer has a passion for what he does even though it is not a very lucrative business. We should not get in the business of pastoring for the money, but because we have been called to reach the lost for Jesus Christ.

A farmer preps the ground for three to four years before he can expect a harvest. He only has a 3 week window to reap the harvest. You must maximize your season. Pastors must continue to preach the Word of God. They must continue to feed their flocks. Pastors must continue to love them and comfort them. When God decides to grow your ministry, you must be ready to reap the harvest. You must aggressively pursue the unchurched so God may bless your life. **Matthew 9:37-38** says, *"(37) Then saith he unto his disciples, The harvest truly is plenteous, but the labourers are few; (38) Pray ye therefore the Lord of the harvest, that he will send forth labourers into his harvest."*

> **Character can keep you where your talents cannot take you.**

Finally, learn from your mistakes. Quit repeating the same mistakes over again. Do not be afraid to try something new. The worst thing that could happen is that project did not work. Pastors invest in your people. Build characters for the long haul. Character can keep you where your talents can not take you.

CHAPTER 8

FOR DISCUSSION

1. What is the greatest enemy of mankind?

2. What is the definition of the "Trinity Rule?"

3. Name and describe how the "Trinity Rule" works.

4. Which third of the "Trinity Rule" will commit to ministry?

5. Describe how the Law of the Harvest works.

6. Will lazy pastors grow a great church for the kingdom? Explain.

7. List seven mistakes you have learned from while pastoring.
   1. _____
   2. _____
   3. _____
   4. _____
   5. _____
   6. _____
   7. _____

8. Why is it so important to invest in people? Explain.

ORDER FORM
Order by phone, fax, mail, or online.

Gary Hawkins Ministries
P.O. Box 870989
Stone Mountain, Georgia 30087
Phone: 770.498.5850   Fax: 770.498.1566
Email: vof@voicesfaith.org   Website: www.voicesfaith.org

QTY	ITEM	EACH	TOTAL
_____	Marketing Your Church for Growth - Book	$12.95	_____
_____	Marketing Your Church for Growth - Audio Cassette	$10.95	_____
_____	Marketing Your Church for Growth - CD	$15.95	_____
_____	Fighting for Your Destiny - Book	$13.95	_____
_____	8 Steps to Prosperity - Book	$15.95	_____
_____	God's Best For Your Life	$15.95	_____
_____	Faith Journal	$10.00	_____
_____	There Is A Word Daily Devotional - Book	Coming Soon	
_____	The Scene Stealer	Coming Soon	
_____	Marketing for Next Level Ministry - Book	$15.95	_____
_____	What Every First Lady Should Know	$14.95	_____
_____	From The Hearts of First Ladies	$15.95	_____
_____	**SUBTOTAL**		_____
_____	Postage and Handling (Call for Shipping Charges)		_____
_____	**TOTAL**		_____

NAME: _____   DATE: _____

ADDRESS: _____   APT./UNIT: _____

CITY: _____ STATE: _____   ZIP: _____

PAYMENT METHOD: ❑ VISA   ❑ MC   ❑ AMEX   ❑ DISCOVER   ❑ CHECK

CREDIT CARD # _____   EXP.: _____

SIGNATURE: _____

About the Author

Gary Hawkins, Sr. is a graduate of Luther Rice Seminary in Lithonia, Georgia. He is the founding pastor of Voices of Faith Ministries in Stone Mountain and Conyers, Georgia. Voices of Faith has seen its membership grow from 75 people to more than 7,000 in only six years. It has been recognized by *Church Growth Magazine* as the 25th fastest growing church in America. Gary Hawkins, Sr. was recognized by *The Church Report Magazine* as one of the top 25 leaders to watch in 2005. Gary and his wife, Debbie, live in Loganville, Georgia with their four children, Elaina, Ashley, Gary Jr. and Kalen.